Pilgrim Prayers for Mealtime

PILGRIM PRAYERS FOR
Mealtime

Alexander Campbell

WIPF & STOCK · Eugene, Oregon

This book is dedicated to the author's two daughters,

Deborah Louise Campbell-Cain

and

Beth Ann Campbell-Maddaluno

who have shown abiding concern and love

for their mother and father all the days of their lives.

Wipf and Stock Publishers
199 W 8th Ave, Suite 3
Eugene, OR 97401

Pilgrim Prayers for Mealtime
By Campbell, Alexander
Copyright©2003 Pilgrim Press
ISBN 13: 978-1-60608-575-2
Publication date 3/27/2009
Previously published by Pilgrim Press, 2003

Contents

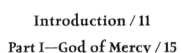

Part IV—God of Love / 57

Part V—God of Peace / 77

Introduction

FROM TIME IMMEMORIAL there have been persons and tribes who have given thanks to a higher power for the food provided by, or for, their well-being. Not only that, gratitude was given for more than food, much more; for sun and rain that the crops might grow; for protection from the elements of nature; and for strength to handle the challenges before them, from sheer survival to meeting day by day situations, large or small.

When persons or families come to the table in our own century to eat the evening meal, many of them pause before a bite is eaten. For some, it has been drilled into them and they give it little thought. They may even wonder why they do it. At any rate, the pause is very brief and they quickly turn to their meal. To some others, who may be more thoughtful, the words of gratitude have, at least, a modicum of meaning. But even for them, if it is the same words repeated day after day after day, the words may eventually grow stale, and the meaning forgotten. I believe there is a better way that can make for a more meaningful situation at the table, and open spiritual horizons that too many persons have not experienced.

Many people say they would like to spend more time with the Bible. But for whatever reason, they just cannot seem to get around to it. Oh yes, we have all heard the statement, "If it is really important you will do it." But what if a lot of things are important to you in an average day in your life? What then? Either you have to cut out something (which can be very difficult to do, sometimes impossible); or find another way to spend time with the Bible, and the guidelines it gives you and family for the living of this life.

Well, there is another way. This other way does not demand an inordinate amount of time. It does not demand finding a separate space in which to do it. And it goes hand in hand with another activity that is rather important in your life: *eating*! What is that other way? It is called *Pilgrim Prayers for Mealtime*.

My reasons for inviting you to explore the contents of this book are threefold:

1. *Pilgrim Prayers for Mealtime* is Bible-based. The scriptures were taken from the Psalms, the Gospels of Matthew, Mark, Luke, John, Romans, I and II Corinthians, Galatians, Ephesians, I and II Timothy, Hebrews, I and II Peter, James, I John, Micah, Isaiah, Proverbs, and Philippians. Thus, we see and hear the words of the ancient Psalmist, of Jesus, and of St. Paul.

2. *Pilgrim Prayers for Mealtime* gives you the opportunity to escape a quick, repetitious, and shallow approach to praying. Instead, you are invited to put your heart and mind and soul into reading or hearing the scripture and in praying to God.

3. *Pilgrim Prayers for Mealtime* highlights one predominant response from beginning to end, *thanksgiving*!

In a few of the devotions, words to that end may not actually be present, but it can be felt. The whole point of taking time before partaking of our food is to give our gratitude to the God who created us; is present with us, and cares for us now and forever.

The book contains devotional graces, each divided into two parts, scripture and prayer. Both the scripture and the prayer are readable by adults, older children, and teens.

To enjoy these devotional graces you may use them in the following ways:

1. One person may do all the reading.

2. More than one person may share in the reading.

3. You begin reading the first devotional grace, then the second, etc., until you reach the last, and then start over again.

4. You do not need to take the devotional graces in sequence if one seems more appropriate for a given circumstance than another.

5. At any time, you might want to take a devotional grace and discuss it at the table, or at a different time and setting. It is up to you.

May God bless and guide you as you begin your journey through the Word of God and through your prayers to God during mealtime.

ONE

God of Mercy

God is Our Refuge

God is our refuge and strength, a very present help in
trouble. Therefore we will not fear, though the earth
should change, though the mountains shake in the
heart of the sea. —Psalm 46:1–2

LET US PRAY

You are our God, and to you we give thanks for your Presence
with us always. When we are afraid, when we are in trouble;
when we do not know quite what to do, we know that you will
strengthen us and guide us. And, thank you this day, O Lord, for
the food that sustains us. In Jesus' name. Amen.

The Earth is the Lord's

The earth is the Lord's and all that is in it, the world,
and those who live in it. —Psalm 24:1

LET US PRAY

We thank you, our God, for the bounty of your world, and for the
food that sustains us. Help us to show our gratitude by the way we
share with the "least of these." In Jesus' name. Amen.

The Lord is My Light

The Lord is my light and my salvation; whom shall I fear? The Lord is the stronghold of my life, of whom shall I be afraid? —PSALM 27:1

LET US PRAY

We give thanks, O Lord, for the inner strength and peace your Spirit brings us. Help us, O God, to take the time to feel you near us. And, thank you for the meal before us. In Jesus' name. AMEN.

Our God be Praised

I will bless the Lord at all times; [God's] praise shall continually be in my mouth. My soul makes its boast in the Lord; let the humble hear and be glad. O magnify the Lord with me, and let us exalt [God's] name together. —PSALM 34:1–3

LET US PRAY

O God, the one and only God, we pause in these moments to bow before you. We come into your Presence in awe, in wonder, and in all humility. You, and you alone, are worthy of our praise and adoration. May we feel your Spirit with us now and forever. In Jesus' name. AMEN.

The Thirst for God

As a deer longs for flowing streams, so my soul longs for you, O God. My soul thirsts for God, for the living God. —Psalm 42:1–2a

LET US PRAY

We thank you God that you do quench the spiritual thirst of those who come to you in spirit and in truth. And we thank you, our God, for the food that gives us strength. In Jesus' name. Amen.

My Rock and My Salvation

For God alone my soul waits in silence; from [God] comes my salvation. [God] alone is my rock and my salvation, my fortress: I shall never be shaken.

—Psalm 62:1–2

LET US PRAY

Almighty God, every good gift comes from you, but none better than the assurance that you are our salvation. And because you are a "rock and fortress" to us, there is nothing we need fear. So, we may live our lives with an inner serenity and peace. The very food that we eat reminds us of your goodness, O God. In Jesus' name. Amen.

A Gracious God

May God be gracious to us and bless us and make [God's] face to shine upon us, that your way may be known upon earth, your saving power among all nations. Let the peoples praise you, O God; let the peoples praise you. —PSALM 67:1–3

LET US PRAY

O Lord, you have been gracious to us in many ways, and you have blessed us beyond our deserving. Now, we would ask your face to shine upon those who need you so much. May they know the food that nourishes. In Jesus' name. AMEN.

A Word of Thanks

We give thanks to you, God; we give thanks; your name is near. People tell of your wondrous deeds.
—PSALM 75:1

LET US PRAY

For health and strength and daily food; for all the joys that make life worth living; for the opportunity to help those who need us so very much, we give you thanks, O God. In Jesus' name. AMEN.

Joy and Rapture

How lovely is your dwelling place, O Lord of hosts. My
soul longs, indeed it faints for the courts of the Lord;
my heart and my flesh sing for joy to the living God.

—PSALM 84:1–2

LET US PRAY

The Psalmist is filled with joy and rapture as he cries out to you,
the living God. Just so, O Lord our God, do we cry out for joy to
you, Creator and Sustainer of our lives. In Jesus' name. AMEN.

Those Who Cry All Day

Incline your ear, O Lord, and answer me,
for I am poor and needy. Preserve my life,
for I am devoted to you; save your servant
who trusts in you. You are my God; be gracious to me,
O Lord, for to you do I cry all day long.

—PSALM 86:1–3

LET US PRAY

Hear our prayer, O God, for those who "cry all day" because they
have little or no food to eat, or safe water to drink. Urge each of us
to do something about it! For Jesus' sake. AMEN.

God's Steadfast Love

I will sing of your steadfast love, O Lord, forever;
with my mouth I will proclaim your faithfulness to
all generations. —Psalm 89:1

LET US PRAY

Even as the table is spread before us, O Lord, so that we can be
nourished, so may we go forth and spread the good news of
your great Love to those who have not really heard it. In Jesus'
name. Amen.

Everlasting to Everlasting

Lord, you have been our dwelling place in all
generations. Before the mountains were brought
forth, or ever you had formed the earth and the
world, from everlasting to everlasting you are God.
                                          —Psalm 90:1–2

LET US PRAY

O God, we give thanks to you for that which makes life possible
in the here and now. Most of all we give thanks for your eternal
Presence with us. In Jesus' name. Amen.

Steadfast Love

It is good to give thanks to the Lord, to sing praises to your name, O Most High; to declare your steadfast love in the morning, and your faithfulness by night.

—PSALM 92:1–2

LET US PRAY

O God, we lift up our voices in song and in speech to you, the One and Almighty God. Thank you, Lord, for every gift given to us, including the food on this table. May we use each gift wisely. In Jesus' name. AMEN.

A Joyful Noise

Make a joyful noise to the Lord, all the earth. Worship the Lord with gladness; come into [God's] presence with singing. Know that the Lord is God. It is [God] that made us, and we are [God's]; we are [God's] people, and the sheep of [God's] pasture.

—PSALM 100:1–3

LET US PRAY

Help us to remember, O God, that you are the Creator, beyond all that we can conceive. And yet you are also closer to us than breathing, ever with us now and forever. Joy! Joy! Joy! In Jesus' name. AMEN.

The Divine Connection

Hear my prayer, O Lord; let my cry come to you. Do not hide your face from me in the day of my distress. Incline your ear to me; answer me speedily in the day when I call. —PSALM 102:1–2

LET US PRAY

Dear God, sometimes we do not feel joyous. Sometimes we feel very low, very depressed, and do not know what to do. Help our spirit connect with your Spirit, so that we may find a way out of our distress, and may feel the joy of your guiding Presence with us. In Jesus' name. AMEN.

All God's Benefits

Bless the Lord, O my soul, and all that is within me, bless [God's] holy name. Bless the Lord, O my soul, and do not forget all [God's] benefits.

—PSALM 103:1–2

LET US PRAY

Gracious God, forgive us for taking all your "benefits" to us for granted. Grant us thankful hearts for all that you have given us; and thank you, Lord, for this food. In Jesus' name. AMEN.

God's Deeds

O give thanks to the Lord, call on [God's] name, make known [God's] deeds among the peoples. Sing to [God], sing praises to [God]; tell of all [God's] wonderful works. —PSALM 105:1–2

Too long, O God, we have kept silent about your presence and love for the lives of all persons. Help us tell them, by words and deeds, so they may know the joy and peace in those who walk with you, O Lord. May they know, in the fullest sense, what it means to eat of the bread of life. In Jesus' name. AMEN.

Praise and Justice

Praise the Lord! O give thanks to the Lord, for [God] is good; for [God's] steadfast love endures forever. Who can utter the mighty doings of the Lord, or declare all [God's] praise? Happy are those who observe justice, who do righteousness at all times.

—PSALM 106:1–3

LET US PRAY

Our God, enable us to treat others in a fair and just way; and to do the right as we have come to know the right. May we give praise and thanksgiving to you every day of our lives. In Jesus' name. AMEN.

Love and Faithfulness

I will give thanks to you, O Lord, among the peoples,
and I will sing praises to you among the nations. For
your steadfast love is higher than the heavens, and
your faithfulness reaches to the clouds.

—Psalm 108:3–4

LET US PRAY

We thank you, O God, for your love that never stops, and for
your faithfulness to us that never diminishes. Thank you, O God,
for the food that nourishes us. In Jesus' name. Amen.

A Sense of Wonder

Blessed be the name of the Lord from this time on and
forevermore. From the rising of the sun to its setting
the name of the Lord is to be praised. The Lord is
high above all nations, and [God's] glory above the
heavens. —Psalm 113:2–4

LET US PRAY

Our God we come before you in humility and with a sense of
wonder. You are more than we can know or imagine. Yet, your
Divine Presence is with us always. Thanks be to you, O God, for
the staff of life. In Jesus' name. Amen.

Walking in God's Way

Happy are those whose way is blameless, who walk in the law of the Lord. Happy are those who keep [God's] decrees, who seek [God] with their whole heart, who also do no wrong, but walk in [God's] ways. —PSALM 119:1–3

LET US PRAY

O God, we confess there are times we do not "walk" in your way. We hurt people close to us, and not so close, by our words and actions. Forgive us, O Lord; help us to speak and act kindly to others, even when it is not easy. In Jesus' name. AMEN.

In the Image of God

I lift up my eyes to the hills—from where will my help come? My help comes from the Lord, who made heaven and earth. —PSALM 121:1–2

LET US PRAY

Dear Lord, at times we forget that you are the Creator and not we, ourselves. You have made us in your own image, giving us the ability to communicate with you, to love others, and to have faith in your Goodness. Thank you, Lord, for all that you mean in our lives. And thank you, Lord, for the food that gives us life. In Jesus' name. AMEN.

In Awe and Wonder

Happy is everyone who fears the Lord, who walks in [God's] ways. You shall eat the fruit of the labor of your hands; you shall be happy, and it shall go well with you. —PSALM 128:1–2

LET US PRAY

Our God, we come before you in awe and wonder. We believe in you, and in your eternal love for us. Strengthen our faith in you, and receive our thanksgiving for the food that keeps us healthy. In Jesus' name. AMEN.

A God Who Listens

Out of the depths I cry to you, O Lord! Lord, hear my voice! Let your ears be attentive to the voice of my supplications! —PSALM 130:1–2

LET US LISTEN

O benevolent Creator, we come to you in all the situations of our lives. Help us to understand that we can bring before you whatever fears, hopes, dreams, and problems we may have, knowing that you, O God, will listen. In Jesus' name. AMEN.

Great is the Lord

I will extol you, my God and King, and bless your
name forever and ever. Every day I will bless you, and
praise your name forever and ever. Great is the Lord,
and greatly to be praised; God's greatness is
unsearchable. —PSALM 145:1–3

LET US PRAY

Dear God, our God, we bow in humility as we consider how
great you are, how wonderful are your works; how abundant is
your goodness. And thank you, God, for the food before us. In
Jesus' name. AMEN.

TWO

God of Grace

Hungry, Homeless, Destitute

Praise the Lord! Praise the Lord, O my soul! I will praise the Lord as long as I live; I will sing praises to my God all my life long. —PSALM 146:1–2

LET US PRAY

Our God, every day of our lives we give thanks to you for your great love for all your people. As we eat of this food, help us to find ways to help your people who are hungry, homeless, and destitute. For Jesus' sake and in his name. AMEN.

Healing the Brokenhearted

Praise the Lord! How good it is to sing praises to our God; for [God] is gracious, and a song of praise is fitting. . . . [God] heals the broken-hearted, and binds up their wounds. . . . The Lord lifts up the downtrodden. —PSALM 147:1, 3, 6

LET US PRAY

O God, we would raise our voices to the very heavens to praise you in speech and in song. And let our actions and empathy reach out to all who are hurting this day, this night. In Jesus' name. AMEN.

With Our Whole Heart

I will give thanks to the Lord with my whole heart; I will tell of all your wonderful deeds. I will be glad and exalt in you; I will sing praise to your name, O Most High. —PSALM 9:1–2

LET US PRAY

May we hear what the Psalmist says, O Lord. May we not be grateful in a halfhearted manner for your goodness to us; but may we, like the Psalmist, "give thanks to the Lord with our whole heart!" In Jesus' name. AMEN.

The Lord is My Rock

I love you, O Lord, my strength. The Lord is my rock, my fortress, and my deliverer, my God, my rock in whom I take refuge, my shield, and the horn of my salvation, my stronghold. —PSALM 18:1–2

LET US PRAY

O God, our God, in you alone we put our trust. You are the Almighty and Eternal One. Your Spirit is with us always. Thank you God for the food that strengthens us. In Jesus' name. AMEN.

Creator and Sustainer

The heavens are telling the glory of God; and the firmament proclaims [God's] handiwork. Day to day pours forth speech, and night to night declares knowledge. —PSALM 19:1–2

LET US PRAY

O God, the skies, the days, the nights, the earth proclaim to all who will hear: that you, our God, is Creator and Sustainer of it all. Thanks be to you forever and ever. In Jesus' name. AMEN.

Confession/Forgiveness

Have mercy on me, O God, according to your steadfast love; according to your abundant mercy blot out my transgressions. Wash me thoroughly from my iniquity, and cleanse me from my sin.

—PSALM 51:1–2

LET US PRAY

O God, we confess to you that we have spoken words and chosen actions that hurt others, both within our family and outside of it. Forgive us, O God, we pray, and help us to treat others with kindness and compassion. In Jesus' name. AMEN.

Humility and Trust

Blessed are the poor in spirit, for theirs is the kingdom of heaven. —MATTHEW 5:3

LET US PRAY

Help us, O God, not to be haughty or arrogant, but to possess within us a humility and a complete trust in you that are marks of citizens of your kingdom. Thank you, Lord, Provider of all things. In Jesus' name. AMEN.

Comfort and Peace

Blessed are those who mourn, for they will be comforted. —MATTHEW 5:4

LET US PRAY

Our God, may these words of Jesus help us to know and to believe, that your Spirit is with us in our most difficult times. May they strengthen us and comfort us and bring us peace. In Jesus' name. AMEN.

Moses was Meek

Blessed are the meek, for they will inherit the earth.

—Matthew 5:5

LET US PRAY

Great Creator of us all, help us to understand that "meek" does not mean weakness or spinelessness. It does mean perseverance and gentleness; also patient and mild. (Moses was described as meek!) Thank you, God, for the meek; and thank you for food that sustains us. In Jesus' name. Amen.

Those Who Hunger

Blessed are those who hunger and thirst for righteousness, for they will be filled. —Matthew 5:6

LET US PRAY

O Divine Providence, through Jesus you remind us that we are called by you to practice rightness and goodness each day of our lives. And, as we eat the meal before us, may we hear your call to feed the hungry, wherever they may be. In Jesus' name. Amen.

Mercy

Blessed are the merciful, for they will receive mercy.
—MATTHEW 5:7

LET US PRAY

Thank you, O God, for your infinite love and mercy. Help us to practice that same love and mercy with others, whomever they may be. So may we receive the mercy promised. In Jesus' name. AMEN.

Pure in Heart

Blessed are the pure in heart, for they will see God.
—MATTHEW 5:8

LET US PRAY

Forgive us, O God, for those times when our thoughts and actions have been anything but pure. May single-minded devotion to you make it possible for us to be clean and true in all our relationships. Thank you for the bread of life, both physical and spiritual. In Jesus' name. AMEN.

Peacemakers

Blessed are the peacemakers, for they will be called children of God. —MATTHEW 5:9

LET US PRAY

O living God, in such a time as now help us to take seriously this piece of scripture. May we not only talk peace, but live it in our daily lives. May we do our part, great or small, to make peace throughout the world between countries, cultures, races, and religions. In Jesus' name. AMEN.

Salt of the Earth

You are the salt of the earth; but if salt has lost its taste, how can its saltiness be restored? It is no longer good for anything, but is thrown out and trampled under foot. —MATTHEW 5:13

LET US PRAY

O Lord, we would be "salt of the earth" persons. We would be preservers of values that are high and holy. We would live lives that are clean and pure. Help us, Lord, to live such a life. And thank you for the table spread; may all your people, Lord, be fed. In Jesus' name. AMEN.

The Light that Shines

You are the light of the world. . . . No one after
lighting a lamp puts it under the bushel basket, but on
the lampstand. . . . In the same way, let your light
shine before others, so that they may see your good
works and give glory to [God] in heaven.

—MATTHEW 5:14–16

LET US PRAY

Our God, too often we feel as if we are engulfed in a great
darkness as we witness the horrible events that make up our
world. Fill us with courage and strength, O God, that we may be
a light that brings truth, peace, justice, and love to all people. In
Jesus' name. AMEN.

Love Your Enemy

You have heard that it was said, "You shall love your neighbor and
hate your enemy." But I say to you, Love your enemies and pray
for those who persecute you. —MATTHEW 5:43–44

LET US PRAY

Our God, we confess that these words of Jesus have been very
difficult for us to follow. We are hurt and want vengeance. But,
Lord, help us also to remember how Jesus forgave those who
killed him. O God, grant us the ability to forgive even when it
seems impossible. In Jesus' name. AMEN.

Treasures in Heaven

Do not store up for yourselves treasures on earth, . . .
where thieves break in and steal; but store up for
yourselves treasures in heaven. . . . For where your
treasure is, there your heart will be also.

—Matthew 6:19–21

LET US PRAY

Dear God, it is so easy for us to think we must have the biggest,
and best, and fastest, and newest. We forget there are so many
who have nothing. O Lord, thank you for our food. And thank
you for all those whose hearts know where their treasure is, and
who help the hurting and the hungry. In Jesus' name. Amen.

Love Others, Love God

No one can serve two masters; for a slave will either
hate the one and love the other, or be devoted to the
one and despise the other. You cannot serve God and
wealth. —Matthew 6:24

LET US PRAY

O God, the God who loves us so much, keep us from worshiping
anyone or anything less than you. May our love for you be shown
by the way we love others in our daily lives. We thank you for the
food that enables us to be your servants to all who need us. In
Jesus' name. Amen.

Persistence

Ask, and it will be given you; search, and you will
find; knock, and the door will be opened for you.
—MATTHEW 7:7

LET US PRAY

Creator and teacher of us all, we confess that all too often we have
had opportunities pass us by because we have not been as
persistent as we should. You tell us that if we try hard enough
good things will happen. Increase our trust in you, O Lord. And
accept our gratitude for the food that gives us energy and
strength. In Jesus' name. AMEN.

The Golden Rule

In everything do to others as you would have them do
to you; for this is the law and the prophets.
—MATTHEW 7:12

LET US PRAY

Our God, how easy it is to say this but so hard to live it. Forgive
us for those times when we have not kept this rule by which to
live. Help us to ask the question: "How would I like others to
treat me?" When we answer that question, O Lord, then help us
to strive to be "Golden Rule" people, empathic people, with all
whom we meet. In Jesus' name. AMEN.

Walk a Good Faith

Not everyone who says to me, "Lord, Lord," will enter the kingdom of heaven, but only the one who does the will of my [parent] in heaven. —MATTHEW 7:21

LET US PRAY

How easy it is, Divine Creator, to talk a good faith instead of act it. In today's language it is easy to talk the walk, but not to walk the walk. We come to you, O God, because we do not want to be hypocrites. We do not want to say one thing and do another. Give us the courage to do your will as we live our lives. Thank you, God, for the food that gives us strength. In Jesus' name. AMEN.

Invitation for Rest

Come to me, all you that are weary and are carrying heavy burdens, and I will give you rest. Take my yoke upon you, and learn from me; for I am gentle and humble in heart, and you will find rest for your souls.
—MATTHEW 11:28–29

LET US PRAY

O God of the universe, yet closer to us than hands or feet, there are times when we are weary in body, mind, and spirit. Some of us are carrying "heavy burdens" and look for the "rest" to which you invite us. Thank you, Lord, for you feed us, and behold, our strength returns. In Jesus' name. AMEN.

Take Up the Cross

Then Jesus told his disciples, "If any want to become my followers, let them deny themselves and take up their cross and follow me. For those who want to save their life will lose it, and those who lose their life for my sake will find it." —MATTHEW 16:24–25

LET US PRAY

Oh, gracious Savior, we know what you have done for us, by going to death on a cross for our sakes. Strengthen our faith and resolve, when tempted to do what we know is wrong, and help us answer the question: WHAT WOULD JESUS DO? In Jesus' name. AMEN.

Forgiving

Then Peter came and said to him, "Lord, if another member of the church sins against me, how often should I forgive? As many as seven times?" Jesus said to him, "Not seven times, but, I tell you, seventy-seven times." —MATTHEW 18:21–22

LET US PRAY

O God, if I have wronged anyone this day, I hope and pray that he or she will forgive me. I also pray that, if anyone has wronged me, I will forgive that person, remembering the words of Jesus. Thank you God for all your mercies. In Jesus' name. AMEN.

Servanthood

Whoever wishes to become great among you must be your servant, and whoever wishes to be first among you must be slave of all. For the Son of [humankind] came not to be served but to serve, and to give his life a ransom for many. —MARK 10:43–45

LET US PRAY

Dear Lord, remind us, that as Christians our ministry must always be to serve others first rather than ourselves. Remind us, also, Lord, that such a ministry begins at the table, as we give thanks to you for the bread of life. In Jesus' name. AMEN.

THREE

God of Thankfulness

The Full Measure of Love

You shall love the Lord your God with all your heart,
and with all your soul, and with all your mind, and
with all your strength. . . . You shall love your neighbor
as yourself. —MARK 12:30–31

LET US PRAY

O God, our God, remind us of what a very wise person said:
"The way you love your neighbor is the way you love God." How
much, O Lord, do we love you? In Jesus' name. AMEN.

Come Like a Child

Jesus called for them and said, "Let the little children
come to me, and do not stop them; for it is to such as
these that the [dominion] of God belongs. Truly I tell
you, whoever does not receive the [dominion] of God
as a little child will never enter it." —LUKE 18:16–17

LET US PRAY

Thank you, O God, for the love, the honesty, the exuberance of a
child. Open our hearts like a child's, that we may be citizens of
your dominion. And thank you, God, for the food that nourishes
us. In Jesus' name. AMEN.

The Light of Life

Again Jesus spoke to them, saying, "I am the light of the world. Whoever follows me will never walk in darkness but will have the light of life." —JOHN 8:12

O Lord, you have given us the light by your teaching, your healing, and your sacrifice. We would stay close to you so that we may walk in "the light of life." As we are about to eat, O God, we pray that the bread of life may be available to all your people. In Jesus' name. AMEN.

The Good Shepherd

I am the good shepherd. I know my own and my own know me, just as [God] knows me and I know [God]. And I lay down my life for the sheep.

—JOHN 10:14-15

LET US PRAY

O Lord Christ, let us never forget that you have laid down your life for our sake. We would be members of your flock, ever open to your leading as we follow you through the pathways and fields of our lives. And when we stumble, Lord, we know that you are there to pick us up and help us on our journey. In your name we pray. AMEN.

The Promise

Jesus said to her, "I am the resurrection and the life. Those who believe in me, even though they die, will live, and everyone who lives and believes in me will never die." —JOHN 11:25–26

LET US PRAY

O Lord Christ, you have given us the promise of life eternal. How do we respond to such a gift? May the lives we live for others, while we are on this earth, be the small way we say, "Thank you, Lord." In Jesus' name. AMEN.

A New Commandment

I give you a new commandment, that you love one another. Just as I have loved you, you also should love one another. By this everyone will know that you are my disciples, if you have love for one another.

—JOHN 13:34–35

LET US PRAY

O God, may we do more than speak love. May we make it the core and cornerstone of the life that we live. Help us, Lord, to be your present-day disciples in love and in truth. And, thank you Lord, for the meal before us. In Jesus' name. AMEN.

Inward Peace

Peace I leave with you; my peace I give to you. I do
not give to you as the world gives. Do not let your
hearts be troubled, and do not let them be afraid.

—JOHN 14:27

LET US PRAY

O God, often the pace of our life is so frantic, and we are filled
with anxieties and problems that are, or seem to be, beyond our
ability to master. Help us to read again, and remember, your
words, that we may know the inward peace that passes
understanding. In Jesus' name. AMEN.

Abide in Me

Abide in me as I abide in you. Just as the branch
cannot bear fruit by itself unless it abides in the vine,
neither can you unless you abide in me. I am the vine,
you are the branches. —JOHN 15:4–5

LET US PRAY

O Lord, as Christians, we think of ourselves as Jesus' disciples.
But, all too often, we neglect your word and get further and
further away from your will for our lives. O Christ, we would
open ourselves to you, that we might "abide in you" and live out
your teachings. Thank you, Lord, for the bread of life. In Jesus'
name. AMEN.

No Separation from God

For I am convinced that neither death, nor life, nor angels, nor rulers, nor things present, nor things to come, nor powers, nor height, nor depth, nor anything else in all creation, will be able to separate us from love of God in Christ Jesus our Lord.

—Romans 8:38–39

LET US PRAY

O God, how wonderful are these words that come to us from St. Paul. They bring us a comfort and peace that guide us through our lives. We give you thanks, Eternal God, that your Spirit is with us now, both in life and in death, and that we will be with you through all eternity. In Jesus' name. Amen.

Actions of Love

Love is patient; love is kind; love is not envious or boastful or arrogant or rude. It does not insist on its own way; it is not irritable or resentful; it does not rejoice in wrongdoing, but rejoices in the truth. It bears all things, believes all things, hopes all things, endures all things. —I Corinthians 13:4–7

LET US PRAY

Dear God, help us to take the message from St. Paul into our daily lives. Let it be for us, not just beautiful words, but actions of love in and through all our relationships with others, whoever they may be. And let it begin around this table here and now. In Jesus' name. Amen.

Think about These Things

Finally, beloved, whatever is true, whatever is
honorable, whatever is just, whatever is pure, whatever
is pleasing, whatever is commendable, if there is any
excellence and if there is anything worthy of praise,
think about these things. —PHILIPPIANS 4:8

LET US PRAY

Our gracious Redeemer, forgive us for all the times that our lives
have not been "worthy of praise." Help us to take a serious look
at ourselves that we may live in harmony with your will for our
lives. Thank you, Lord, for the food that sustains and the spiritual
guidance you give us through all our life. In Jesus' name. AMEN.

God the Protector

Protect me, O God, for in you I take refuge. I say to
the Lord, "You are my Lord; I have no good apart
from you." —PSALM 16:1–2

LET US PRAY

O God and Creator of us all, help us to understand that you are
always there for us, no matter how hard our life is. And although
we cannot see you with our eyes, we can, if we will, feel your
comforting Presence with us. And, we know that nothing can ever
separate us from you. Receive our thanks for this food and for your
everlasting love. In Jesus' name. AMEN.

The Lord is My Shepherd

The Lord is my shepherd, I shall not want. [God] makes me lie down in green pastures; and leads me beside still waters. —PSALM 23:1–2

LET US PRAY

Great and gentle Shepherd, we need you with us so much. When we are hurting, or tired, or anxious let us feel you very near us. Help us feel the "green pastures" of your love and the "still waters" of your peace. In Jesus' name. AMEN.

Lead Me in Your Truth

Make me to know your ways, O Lord; teach me your paths. Lead me in your truth, and teach me, for you are the God of my salvation; for you I wait all day long. —PSALM 25:4–5

LET US PRAY

Our Lord and our Teacher, may we open our hearts and minds, our eyes and ears, so that we may know and practice the truth every day of our lives. Thank you for the food that makes us strong, and for the truth that makes us free. In Jesus' name. AMEN.

Our Soul Waits for the Lord

Our soul waits for the Lord; [God] is our help and
shield. Our heart is glad in [the Lord], because we
trust in [God's] holy name. Let your steadfast love, O
Lord, be upon us, even as we hope in you.

—PSALM 33:20–22

LET US PRAY

Our infinite and caring God, we rejoice with great joy knowing
that we are not adrift, all alone, with no one who cares for us or
loves us. We have you, and all the people who trust in you, who
are there to care and to love us. O God, make us messengers of
your love to those who need that love; and givers of food to those
who need it, so they may live. In Jesus' name. AMEN.

Humans and Animals Alike

Your steadfast love, O Lord, extends to the heavens,
your faithfulness to the clouds. Your righteousness is
like the mighty mountains, your judgments are like
the great deep; you save humans and animals alike, O
Lord. —PSALM 36:5–6

LET US PRAY

O Great Creator, you remind us through the Psalmist that you
love and care not only for the humans you have created; you also
remind us that you love the animals, big and small, that you have
created. Help us to understand that when we care for them, we
do your will. In Jesus' name. AMEN.

Waiting Patiently

I waited patiently for the Lord; [God] inclined to me
and heard my cry. . . . [The Lord] put a new song in
my mouth, a song of praise to our God.

—PSALM 40:1, 3A

LET US PRAY

How many times, O Lord, have we made a request of you and
when it was not given quickly, walked, sadly, away. Help us, O
Lord, to practice patience, knowing that in your good time, the
answer will come. Thank you for the food before us, O Great
Giver of all gifts. In Jesus' name. AMEN.

Songs of Joy

Clap your hands, all you peoples; shout to God with
loud songs of joy. For the Lord, the Most High, is
awesome, a great king over all the earth.

—PSALM 47:1–2

LET US PRAY

Our God, remind us that our faith is a source of joy, rather than
gloom and doom. In the word so long ago that is hip today, you,
Great God, are "awesome!" So, may we clap our hands and still
sing joyous songs to you, O Lord, for you are, indeed, Most
High! In Jesus' name. AMEN.

All Creatures Belong to God

For every wild animal of the forest is mine, the cattle on a thousand hills. I know all the birds of the air, and all that moves in the field is mine. —PSALM 50:10–11

LET US PRAY

How precious are all that you have made O Wondrous Creator! How precious in your sight is the smallest of creatures and animals of great size. You, O God, have given them into our hands to care for, to treat kindly, and never to abuse. Thank you, O Lord, for these special creatures on our earth. In Jesus' name. AMEN.

Love and Faithfulness

I will give thanks to you, O Lord, among the peoples; I will sing praises to you among the nations. For your steadfast love is as high as the heavens; your faithfulness extends to the clouds. —PSALM 57:9–10

LET US PRAY

You have decreed, O Lord, what is central to the life of one who would be a follower, a disciple, a Christian: love and faithfulness. More and more, O Lord, may they be at the core of our lives; and may others be blessed because they are. Thank you, God, for the staff of life. In Jesus' name. AMEN.

My Soul Thirsts for You

O God, you are my God, I seek you, my soul thirsts for you; my flesh faints for you, as in a dry and weary land where there is no water. —PSALM 63:1

LET US PRAY

O God, our God, sometimes we know what it means to want a cold drink of water because our mouths are dry, and we are very tired. And, oh, what a wonderful feeling when our mouths drink of that cool, refreshing water and we feel alive again. Just so, our God, would we seek you, be close to you, and in word and action, feel alive as your true disciples. In Jesus' name. AMEN.

God of Mercy

In you, O Lord, I take refuge; let me never be put to shame. In your righteousness deliver me and rescue me; incline your ear to me and save me. Be to me a rock of refuge, a strong fortress, to save me, for you are my rock and my fortress. —PSALM 71:1–3

LET US PRAY

O God who saves, help us to put our undying faith in you and in your unending love for your people. You, and you alone, O God, are our Rock of refuge and the Giver of our hope. Thank you for giving us the food that sustains us; and Source of all mercy, use us to feed those of your children who need that food for life itself. In Jesus' name. AMEN.

You Hold My Right Hand

I am continually with you; you hold my right hand. . . .
Whom have I in heaven but you? And there is nothing
on earth that I desire other than you. My flesh and my
heart may fail, but God is the strength of my heart and
my portion forever. —PSALM 73:23, 25–26

LET US PRAY

God of eternal light, the Psalmist reminds us of an eternal truth:
your faithfulness to us never fails. Even when we are unaware of it,
your Guiding Presence is with us always; but we must be open in
mind and heart to receive it. Help us, each of us, to put our hand
in yours, Guide of all humanity. In Jesus' name. AMEN.

I Cry Aloud to God

I cry aloud to God . . . that [God] may hear me. In the
day of my trouble I seek the Lord; in the night my hand
is stretched out without wearying; my soul refuses to be
comforted. —PSALM 77:1–2

LET US PRAY

God of all Comfort, life is not always good for us, your people,
young and old. There are so many who live in darkness, doubt, and
helplessness. We pray, O God that such as these may reach out to
you for comfort. And, if comfort does not come to them right
away, give them the patience and the faith they need, so that they
may know your guiding Presence is with them now and always.
Thank you, O God, for the food that gives life to all. In Jesus'
name. AMEN.

The People of God's Pasture

O come, let us worship and bow down, let us kneel before the Lord, our Maker! For [the Lord] is our God, and we are the people of [God's] pasture, and the sheep of [God's] hand.—PSALM 95:6–7

LET US PRAY

God of holiness, we come into your presence in humility and awe. You are our God, and you have made us, and not we, ourselves. So, we kneel before you. And in these moments we would have a deep sense of your Spiritual Presence with us, in this world and in your dominion come. In Jesus' name. AMEN.

FOUR

God of Love

Sing to the Lord

O sing to the Lord a new song; sing to the Lord, all
the earth. Sing to the Lord, bless [God's] name; tell of
[God's] salvation from day to day. Declare [God's]
glory among the nations, [God's] marvelous works
among all the peoples. —PSALM 96:1–3

LET US PRAY

High and Holy One, it is good to hear the Psalmist as he shouts
of a new song, a song that should be heard throughout the earth.
Let all the nations hear the song, catch the overflowing joy, and
exalt you, God of our salvation! From you, O Lord, comes food,
blessing, and your Spirit with us always. In Jesus' name. AMEN.

Pity on the Weak

For [God] delivers the needy when they call, the poor
and those who have no helper. [God] has pity on the
weak and the needy, and saves the lives of the needy.
—PSALM 72:12–13

LET US PRAY

Judge of all humankind, we bow our heads in your Presence, as
we confess the times when we could have reached out to those in
need and did not go out of our way to do it. Forgive us, O God,
and help us to walk in your footsteps, as we feed and serve the
needy, the weak, and the poor. In Jesus' name. AMEN.

The Earth is Full of God's Creatures

O Lord, how manifold are your works! In wisdom you have made them all; the earth is full of your creatures. Yonder is the sea, great and wide, creeping things innumerable are there, living things both small and great. —PSALM 104:24–25

LET US PRAY

Creator of all, we are reminded that you have made us, male and female, in your image. And you have given us the responsibility of taking wise and loving care of the creatures you have created. Guide us in this very important task. In Jesus' name. AMEN.

Gracious, Merciful, and Righteous

Praise the Lord! Happy are those who fear the Lord,
who greatly delight in [God's] commandments. . . .
They rise in the darkness as a light for the upright;
they are gracious, merciful and righteous. . . . They
have distributed freely, they have given to the poor;
their righteousness endures forever. —PSALM 112:1, 4, 9

LET US PRAY

O Giver of all good things, we give you thanks for the verbal
picture from the Psalmist of those who are really and truly
upright. They walk the earth as those who know what it is to do
your will, O God. May your blessing rest upon all those who
follow in their footsteps. Thank you, Lord, for food that energizes
us and keeps us well. In Jesus' name. AMEN.

The Love that Endures Forever

You are my God, and I will give thanks to you; you are
my God, I will extol you. O give thanks to the Lord,
who is good, for [God's] steadfast love endures forever.
—PSALM 118:28–29

O God, forgive us for those times when we have forgotten you,
going about our daily routines as if you did not exist. Remind us,
O Lord, that you are the One to give us life; you are the One who
walks with us through all our days; and you are the One who
loves us now and eternally. In the words of the Psalmist: "You are
our God, and we will extol you!" In Jesus' name. AMEN.

The Blessedness of Unity

How very good and pleasant it is when kindred live
together in unity! It is like the precious oil on the
head, running down upon the beard, on the beard of
Aaron, running down over the collar of his robes.
—PSALM 133:1–2

LET US PRAY

God of all generations, how sad it is to see families broken,
kindred at odds with one another, and hurtful words and actions
the norm. But, O God, may the eyes of all be opened and
forgiveness and understanding of each other reign. So, may they
find how good and blessed it is to live in unity. And, God of holy
love, hear our gratitude for the food that sustains us. In Jesus'
name. AMEN.

The Everywhere of God

Where can I go from your spirit? Or where can I flee
from your presence? If I ascend to heaven, you are
there; if I make my bed in Sheol, you are there. If I
take the wings of the morning and settle at the farthest
limits of the sea, even there your hand shall lead me,
and your right hand shall hold me fast.

—Psalm 139:7–10

LET US PRAY

God of earth and air, height and depth, the God of everywhere,
how foolish it is to try and hide ourselves from you. There is
nowhere that you are not; and, most important of all, there is
nowhere that your all-encompassing love does not surround us. It
is good to know that "your right hand shall hold me fast." In
Jesus' name. AMEN.

The Justice of God

I know that the Lord maintains the cause of the needy,
and executes justice for the poor. Surely the righteous
shall give thanks to your name; the upright shall live
in your presence. —PSALM 140:12–13

LET US PRAY

Protector of all who trust, we know that you have special
compassion for the weak and the poor. And that you have harsh
justice for those who are rich and powerful at the expense of the
poor. May the eyes of those who exploit the needy be open; may
they repent their actions; and may your trusting people, O Lord
of mercy, come to find a better and happier life. In Jesus'
name. AMEN.

O That Big Mouth

Set a guard over my mouth, O Lord; keep watch over
the door of my lips. Do not turn my heart to any evil,
to busy myself with wicked deeds. —PSALM 141:3–4A

LET US PRAY

O Lord, how much trouble these mouths of ours can cause. How
much pain and hurt we can inflict when we do not carefully
"watch over the door of our lips." Forgive us. O God. Help us to
speak in ways that communicate love and tenderness and good
feelings to others. And, thank you, Lord, for the energizing food
that comes into our mouths each day. In Jesus' name. AMEN.

Praise the Lord

Praise the Lord! Praise the Lord, O my soul! I will praise the Lord as long as I live; I will sing praises to my God all my life long. —Psalm 146:1–2

LET US PRAY

O God of all goodness. O Giver of salvation! O Great Healer of body and soul. O Source of life. O Source of truth and law. O Almighty God of heaven and earth. All this and so much more you mean to us. And, so we say what the Psalmist of old said so long ago: "Praise the Lord! Praise the Lord, O my soul!" For all that you mean to us this day and all our days, we praise you, O loving and holy and forgiving God. In Jesus' name. Amen.

In the Beginning

In the beginning was the Word, and the Word was with God, and the Word was God. He was in the beginning with God. All things came into being through him, and without him not one thing came into being. —John 1:1–3

LET US PRAY

Almighty Creator of heaven and earth we bow before you as we attempt to comprehend the immensity of all your creation. We know that you expect us to care for your creation in ways that are in harmony with your will and that will benefit all people and all your beloved creatures. Grant us the knowledge and the motivation to do so. Thank you Lord for the food that gives us strength. In Jesus' name. Amen.

God So Loved the World

For God so loved the world that [God] gave an only
Son, so that everyone who believes in [Jesus] may not
perish but may have eternal life. Indeed, God did not
send the Son into the world to condemn the world,
but in order that the world might be saved through
him. —JOHN 3:16–17

LET US PRAY

God of hope and joy, you make it so very clear to us why Jesus
came into this world. As a teacher, as a healer, as a storyteller, and
as one willing to sacrifice himself on a cruel cross, he came to
offer an invitation to a new life. All that was needed was a
complete trust in all that Jesus stood for. To such belongs the life
that is eternal. Thank you, Giver of all good things, for such a
precious gift. In Jesus' name. AMEN.

In Spirit and In Truth

But the hour is coming, and is now here, when the
true worshipers will worship [God] in spirit and in
truth, for [God] seeks such as these to worship. God is
spirit, and those who worship [God] must worship in
spirit and in truth. —JOHN 4:23–24

LET US PRAY

O God, we hear Jesus as he reminds the woman, with whom he
was in conversation, of the nature of true worship. It is not of all
importance where and when persons worship. What is important
is how we worship, said Jesus. We are to worship you, O God, in
spirit and in truth. Help us, O Lord, to worship in love, in
humility, in honesty, and with an open mind and heart. In Jesus'
name. AMEN.

The Bread of Life

This is the bread that comes down from heaven, so that one may eat of it and not die. I am the living bread that came down from heaven. Whoever eats of this bread will live forever; and the bread that I will give for the life of the world is my flesh. —JOHN 6:50–51

LET US PRAY

God of the morning, noon, and evening of our lives, you have made possible the development of our lives through what the earth provides for us. We thank you for our daily bread. But, we also give unending gratitude to you, O God, for Jesus' promise that we may eat of the bread that is eternal, which he gave "for the life of the world." Praise be to you, O God, from whom all blessings flow. In Jesus' name. AMEN.

The Light of the World

Again Jesus spoke to them, saying, "I am the light of the world. Whoever follows me will never walk in darkness but will have the light of life." —JOHN 8:12

LET US PRAY

O gracious God, your Son, Jesus, is the light of the world. How great it is to know that if we are true disciples of the Christ that we, too, are people of the light: people of goodness, of love, of humility, of faith in their God. Thank you, O Lord, for such a gift. And, thank you also, Lord, for the meals that give us life. In Jesus' name. AMEN.

I Am the Good Shepherd

I am the good shepherd. I know my own and my own know me, just as [God] knows me and I know [God]. And I lay down my life for the sheep. —JOHN 10:14–15

LET US PRAY

We are reminded in this passage, Source of deliverance and help, of what it is that keeps the ninety-nine sheep from straying away, of following the shepherd's lead wherever he goes. It is because they trust the shepherd fully and completely. Do we trust you as fully and completely as the sheep trusts the shepherd? Help us O God, to trust you with our life each day. In Jesus' name. AMEN.

The Resurrection and the Life

Jesus said to her, "I am the resurrection and the life. Those who believe in me, even though they die, will live, and everyone who lives and believes in me will never die." —JOHN 11:25–26

LET US PRAY

One and eternal God, our hearts are filled with unspeakable joy as we hear the reply of Jesus in conversation with a lady named Martha. We remember that Jesus raised her brother Lazarus from the dead. And now Jesus assures her that all those who "live and believe in me will never die." Help us all understand, Almighty God, that the promise of everlasting life that comes from the lips of Jesus is meant for now and forever. Thank you, Keeper of our souls, for a joy that has no end! In Jesus' name. AMEN.

A New Commandment

I give you a new commandment, that you love one another. Just as I have loved you, you also should love one another. By this everyone will know that you are my disciples, if you have love for one another.

—John 13:34–35

LET US PRAY

Sometimes, God of all goodness, you know it is not always easy to love someone, especially if that person has hurt you. Yet, Jesus knew how important it was for his disciples to love one another. If they showed that love others would see it, and they would want to be followers of this new faith. So, he "commanded" them to do it! Give us the courage, Lord, to love others when it is hard to do. In Jesus' name. Amen.

The Way, the Truth, the Life

Jesus said to him, "I am the way, and the truth, and the life. . . . If you know me, you will know my [parent] also. From now on you do know [God] and have seen [God]." —JOHN 14:6–7

LET US PRAY

Thank you, O God, for sending Jesus to live among us. His being with us has meant more than we can ever think or imagine. One thing that Jesus has done for us is reveal who and what You, O God, are like. And the answer is so simple: *Who Jesus was, O God, you are!* As Jesus told his disciples: "If you know me, you will know my [parent] also." Thanks be to you, O God, forever and ever. And thank you for the food that strengthens us. In Jesus' name. AMEN.

Peace

Peace I leave with you; my peace I give to you. I do
not give to you as the world gives. Do not let your
hearts be troubled, and do not let them be afraid.

—JOHN 14:27

LET US PRAY

God of peace, hear us as we call upon you. Those who are caught
in the upheavals between and within nations, are searching
frantically for peace. And, O Lord, we also pray for peace of heart
and mind for those who mourn, who are ill, who are fighting
poverty, or fighting drugs, or cancer, or HIV/AIDS, or any other
malady. We pray for them that they may overcome with the help
of those who care. And through Jesus they may know the peace
that passes understanding. In Jesus' name. AMEN.

For One's Friends

This is my commandment, that you love one another as I have loved you. No one has greater love than this, to lay down one's life for one's friends. —JOHN 15:12–13

God of Holy Love, we listen to the words that Jesus speaks about giving one's life for a friend. We remember how he gave his life, not only for his disciples, but for us all. And, we remember, O God, those who have given their lives so that others might live in peace and security in the land they love. Help us, never to forget their courage and their love. In Jesus' name. AMEN.

Take Courage

The hour is coming, indeed it has come, when you
will be scattered, each one to [their] home, and you
will leave me alone. Yet I am not alone because [God]
is with me. I have said this to you, so that in me you
may have peace. In the world you face persecution.
But take courage; I have conquered the world!

—JOHN 16:32–33

LET US PRAY

Eternal Spirit of the Universe, may we have that same sense of your
nearness to us that Jesus had. Sometimes we, too, feel very much
alone. Help us, O God, to remember: In his turmoil Jesus had you,
ever close by. The world can be tough; but we have you God, with
us all the way and all the day. As Jesus said: "take courage; I have
conquered the world!" In Jesus' name. AMEN.

Life In His Name

Now Jesus did many other signs in the presence of his disciples, which are not written in this book. But these are written so that you may come to believe that Jesus is the Messiah, the Son of God, and that through believing you may have life in his name. —JOHN 20:30–31

LET US PRAY

Thank you, O great and wonderful God, for the purpose that was behind the writing of the Gospel of John. It was that we might "believe that Jesus is the Messiah, the Son of God, and that through believing you may have life in his name." A life of meaning and purpose here and now. Yet, also, a life beyond this one in the dominion of God. Thanks be to you, O God, forever and ever for such an incredible gift! In Jesus' name. AMEN.

The Truth Will Make You Free

Then Jesus said to the Jews who had believed in him, "If you continue in my word, you are truly my disciples; and you will know the truth, and the truth will make you free." —JOHN 8:31–32

LET US PRAY

God of truth, how difficult it often seems in our day to know what is truth and what is not truth. How do we choose? Thank you, God for giving us the answer: the life and teachings and sacrifice of Jesus Christ. That is the norm by which, if we are Christian, truth is judged. That is the norm by which we live our lives. Thank you, O God, for sharing that norm with us. Thank you God for sharing this food with us. In Jesus' name. AMEN.

The Holy Spirit

And suddenly from heaven there came a sound like the rush of a violent wind, and it filled the entire house where they were sitting. Divided tongues, as of fire, appeared among them, and a tongue rested on each of them. All of them were filled with the Holy Spirit and began to speak in other languages, as the Spirit gave them ability. —ACTS 2:2–4

LET US PRAY

Eternal Spirit, we confess before you that we talk and think very little about you. Help us to feel the power of your Spirit, the Holy Spirit, as did the disciples so long ago. O Holy Spirit of God, may we open our hearts and our minds, so that you will be real to us as we live our lives. In Jesus' name. AMEN.

FIVE

God of Peace

Repentance and Baptism

Peter said to them, "Repent, and be baptized every one of you in the name of Jesus Christ so that your sins may be forgiven; and you will receive the gift of the Holy Spirit." . . . They devoted themselves to the apostles' teaching and fellowship, to the breaking of bread and the prayers. —ACTS 2:38, 42

LET US PRAY

God of grace and glory, what a day that must have been when your Holy Spirit empowered the apostles. Oh, to have been there when three thousand people repented and were baptized in the name of Jesus Christ. And, so the Christian Church had its beginning! O God, may we be worthy to have your spirit come into our lives. And, thank you, Lord, for the food that nourishes. In Jesus' name. AMEN.

Justified by Faith

Therefore, since we are justified by faith, we have
peace with God through our Lord Jesus Christ,
through whom we have obtained access to this grace
in which we stand; and we boast in our hope of
sharing the glory of God. —ROMANS 5:1–2

LET US PRAY

We thank you, O Gracious God, for the gift of being called "the
children of God." You forgive us our sins; you open to us a whole
new life; you reconcile us through the sacrifice of Jesus Christ;
you help us walk in the way of goodness. And all we need to do is
to put our trust fully and joyously in you, O God of everlasting
love. In Jesus' name. AMEN.

The Spirit Helps Us

Likewise the Spirit helps us in our weakness; for we do
not know how to pray as we ought, but that very
Spirit intercedes with sighs too deep for words.
                                    —ROMANS 8:26

LET US PRAY

O Patient God, how often we come to you and we want to lay
our innermost thoughts before you, but we do not know how to
do it. Help us to feel your Spirit very close to us, enabling us to
find the words we want, to express the thoughts we have. Teach
us patience, O Lord, for you know our thoughts before we ever
utter them. And, thank you Lord, for the meal before us. In Jesus'
name. AMEN.

More than Conquerors

Who will separate us from the love of Christ? Will hardship, or distress, or persecution, or famine, or nakedness, or peril, or sword? . . . No, in all these things we are more than conquerors through [the One] who loved us. For I am convinced that neither death, nor life, nor angels, nor rulers, nor things present, nor things to come, nor powers, nor height, nor depth, nor anything else in all creation, will be able to separate us from the love of God in Christ Jesus our Lord. —ROMANS 8:35, 37–39

LET US PRAY

O God of ages past and present, we are humbled and in awe as we read, and listen to, these words from St. Paul. It is a virtual song of faith, a song that inspires us to embrace every thought within it. O God, may such a faith be, and continue, in us through all the days of our lives. In Jesus' name. AMEN.

Marks of the True Christian

Let love be genuine; hate what is evil, hold fast to
what is good; love one another with mutual affection;
outdo one another in showing honor. Do not lag in
zeal, be ardent in spirit, serve the Lord. Rejoice in
hope, be patient in suffering, persevere in prayer.
Contribute to the needs of the saints; extend
hospitality to strangers. —ROMANS 12:9–13

LET US PRAY

God of health and salvation, we thank you for the ways that St.
Paul presents to us the "Marks of the True Christian." Help us to
follow what he sets before us, by both word and deed, in our
daily living. Let us remember, Lord God, that it is not enough
just to say we believe in Jesus; but to demonstrate it by the kind
of lives we live. In Jesus' name. AMEN.

Love One Another

Owe no one anything, except to love one another; for the one who loves another has fulfilled the law. The commandments, "You shall not commit adultery; You shall not murder; You shall not steal; You shall not covet"; and any other commandment, are summed up in this word, "Love your neighbor as yourself."

—Romans 13:8–9

LET US PRAY

Giver of Love, we thank you for this message from your servant, Paul. We hear him telling us that of all the good things, of all nice things, of all the important things we can do in relationship to our neighbors is to love them. To love them in such a way as we would want to be loved by them. And, to do so, even if it is difficult to do! O God, grant us the strength to make it so. May we approach this table with gratitude for the bread of life. In Jesus' name. Amen.

Jesus Christ, Crucified

When I came to you, brothers and sisters, I did not come proclaiming the mystery of God to you in lofty words or wisdom. For I decided to know nothing among you except Jesus Christ, and him crucified.

—I CORINTHIANS 2:1–2

LET US PRAY

Eternal Source of knowledge, how grateful we are that your message to us through Paul, and others, can be delivered in simple, everyday words. That the story of Jesus, crucified, can be told in such a way, that the wonder of his coming can be understood and accepted by all. Help us, O Lord, so that we can give our own witness of Christ to others who need to hear it. In Jesus' name. AMEN.

The Resurrection of the Dead

So it is with the resurrection of the dead. What is
sown is perishable, what is raised is imperishable. It is
sown in dishonor, it is raised in glory. It is sown in
weakness, it is raised in power. It is sown a physical
body, it is raised a spiritual body. If there is a physical
body, there is also a spiritual body. . . . But thanks be
to God, who gives us the victory through our Lord
Jesus Christ. —I CORINTHIANS 15:42–44, 57

LET US PRAY

God of life and death, we put our trust fully and completely in
you. We do not know, O Eternal God, about the spiritual realm.
But we have your promise through Jesus that all who believe in
him will have everlasting life. "Praise be to you, O God, who
gives us the victory through our Lord Jesus Christ." In Jesus'
name. AMEN.

The Greatest of These is Love

Love is patient; love is kind; love is not envious or
boastful or arrogant or rude. It does not insist on its
own way; it is not irritable or resentful; it does not
rejoice in wrongdoing, but rejoices in the truth. It
bears all things, believes all things, hopes all things,
endures all things. . . . And now faith, hope and love
abide, these three; and the greatest of these is love.

—I CORINTHIANS 13:4–7, 13

LET US PRAY

God of holy love, your love is beyond all that we can think or
imagine. It is a love that asks nothing in return; a love for us even
when we are undeserving of it. It invites us to spend time reading
and re-reading I Corinthians 13, and then practicing in our own
lives what love really means. In Jesus' name. AMEN.

In the One Spirit

For just as the body is one and has many members,
and all the members of the body, though many, are
one body, so it is with Christ. For in the one Spirit we
were all baptized into one body—Jews or Greeks,
slaves or free—and we were all made to drink of one
Spirit. —I Corinthians 12:12–13

LET US PRAY

Creator and Preserver of all humankind, you love all that you
have created with an equal love. All are precious in your sight. In
our churches there are many members of many races, faiths, and
nationalities. And all the members are needed. Help us to
remember, O God of the universe, we are one in Christ, baptized
as one in the Spirit. Thanks be to God! In Jesus' name. Amen.

The Fruit of the Spirit

By contrast, the fruit of the Spirit is love, joy, peace, patience, kindness, generosity, faithfulness, gentleness, and self-control. There is no law against such things. . . . If we live by the Spirit, let us also be guided by the Spirit. Let us not become conceited, competing against one another, envying one another.

—GALATIANS 5:22–23, 25–26

LET US PRAY

Creator of all goodness and beauty, we would give ourselves to the practice of the "fruit of the Spirit." In our daily lives we would try, as difficult as it might sometimes be, to walk in the steps of Jesus. We know, Spirit of God, that you will be with us as we attempt to live the life Paul sets out before us. Thank you, our God, for such gifts as these, and for the food upon this table. In Jesus' name. AMEN.

Breaking Down the Wall

But now in Christ Jesus you who once were far off have been brought near by the blood of Christ. For he is our peace; in his flesh he has made both groups into one and has broken down the dividing wall, that is, the hostility between us. —EPHESIANS 2:13–14

LET US PRAY

God of peace, we need your Presence with us in a time when hostilities are so rampant all over our world. Hostilities between individuals, nations, cultures, religions, and others. Hostilities that have the direst consequences, even death itself. O God, may we, who claim devotion to the sacrifice of Jesus, give ourselves in this day to the breaking down of walls and to the birth of peace. In Jesus' name. AMEN.

Rooted and Grounded in Love

I pray that . . . [God] may grant that you may be
strengthened in your inner being with power through
[the] Spirit, and that Christ may dwell in your hearts
through faith, as you are being rooted and grounded
in love. . . . and to know the love of Christ that
surpasses knowledge, so that you may be filled with all
the fullness of God. —EPHESIANS 3:16–17, 19

LET US PRAY

O Faithful God, how beautiful, how compelling are the wishes of
the apostle for the people in the church at Ephesus. And, now,
two thousand years later, when we read and hear these words, we
have a very strong sense that they are meant for us as well. For
we, too, would "know the love of Christ that surpasses
knowledge;" and we, too, would "be filled with all the fullness of
God." Thanks be to you, O Lord, for this spiritual gift. Accept,
also, our gratitude for this nourishment. In Jesus' name. AMEN.

One Body and One Spirit

I, therefore, the prisoner in the Lord, beg you to lead a life worthy of the calling to which you have been called, with all humility and gentleness, with patience, bearing with one another in love, making every effort to maintain the unity of the Spirit in the bond of peace. There is one body and one Spirit, just as you were called to the one hope of your calling, one Lord, one faith, one baptism, one God and [parent] of all, who is above all and through all and in all.

—EPHESIANS 4:1–6

LET US PRAY

O Searcher of hearts, it is to our hearts that these words speak. We listen and we are quiet. (Pause.) Thank you, O God, for these very special words; and for the food that sustains us. In Jesus' name. AMEN.

Speaking the Truth in Love

We must no longer be children, tossed to and fro and
blown about by every wind of doctrine, by people's
trickery, by their craftiness in deceitful scheming. But
speaking the truth in love, we must grow up in every
way into him who is the head, into Christ.

—EPHESIANS 4:14–15

LET US PRAY

Our Creator and our Teacher, we remember that Jesus advised his
disciples when they were about to go on a special mission: "See, I
am sending you out like sheep into the midst of wolves; so be
wise as serpents and innocent as doves" (Matthew 10:16).
Likewise, the folk in Paul's time; likewise, ourselves in our time.
O God, when we speak, may we speak the truth, as we know it,
but do our best to speak it in love. In Jesus' name. AMEN.

Be Kind to One Another

Put away from you all bitterness and wrath and anger
and wrangling and slander, together with all malice,
and be kind to one another, tenderhearted, forgiving
one another, as God in Christ has forgiven you.

—Ephesians 4:31–32

LET US PRAY

O God, we pause to think about these words written to the
church at Ephesus so many years ago. O Lord, those who were
guilty of such words and actions must have the felt the sting of
the apostle's words. In the church of our time do we feel the
sting, also? O gracious God, grant us a sense of caring so that we
may reach out in kindness to all the members of our church and
community. In Jesus' name. Amen.

The Shield of Faith

Stand therefore, and fasten the belt of truth around your waist, and put on the breastplate of righteousness. As shoes for your feet, put on whatever will make you ready to proclaim the gospel of peace. With all of these, take the shield of faith, with which you will be able to quench all the flaming arrows of the evil one. Take the helmet of salvation, and the sword of the Spirit, which is the word of God.

—EPHESIANS 6:14–17

LET US PRAY

O God, the God of all goodness and faithfulness, we would give you thanks for these words; words that spell out what a Christian is really like. O Lord, let us, in our hearts, meditate on what these words tell us about who we can be. And, thank you, Lord, for meeting our hunger at this table. In Jesus' name. AMEN.

Jesus Christ is Lord

Let the same mind be in you that was in Christ Jesus, who, though he was in the form of God, did not regard equality with God as something to be exploited, but emptied himself, taking the form of a slave, being born in human likeness. And being found in human form, he humbled himself and became obedient to the point of death—even death on a cross. Therefore God also highly exalted him and gave him the name that is above every name, so that at the name of Jesus every knee should bend, in heaven and on earth and under the earth, and every tongue should confess that Jesus Christ is Lord, to the glory of God.

—Philippians 2:5–11

LET US PRAY

O God, made manifest in Jesus Christ our Lord, let these words dwell within us deeply. Let them speak to our very souls. All glory to you, O God most high. In Jesus' name. Amen.

Think about These Things

Finally, beloved, whatever is true, whatever is
honorable, whatever is just, whatever is pure, whatever
is pleasing, whatever is commendable, if there is any
excellence and if there is anything worthy of praise,
think about these things. Keep on doing the things
that you have learned and received and heard and seen
in me, and the God of peace will be with you.

—PHILIPPIANS 4:8–9

LET US PRAY

Gracious God, we thank you that through Paul you share with us,
in these verses, some of what it takes to live as a Christian:
speaking what is true; acting honorably; doing that which is just;
living pure lives; and trying, humbly, to do Your will, O God of
our salvation. May that be our goal, O loving God, each day of
our lives. In Jesus' name. AMEN.

A Good Minister of Jesus Christ

Let no one despise your youth, but set the believers an example in speech and conduct, in love, in faith, in purity. Until I arrive, give attention to the public reading of scripture, to exhorting, to teaching. Do not neglect the gift that is in you, which was given to you through prophecy with the laying on of hands by the council of elders.—I TIMOTHY 4:12–14

LET US PRAY

God of all generations, remind us that you not only work through adults; that you also work through the young people of our time. Even as Paul gave instructions to Timothy so long ago, we know, O Lord, that you give the same basic instructions to all young people of this century who wish to serve you. May they hear the same words as did Timothy: "Do not neglect the gift that is in you." Enable them, O Lord, to find that special gift that is theirs. In Jesus' name. AMEN.

The Love of Money

But those who want to be rich fall into temptation
and are trapped by many senseless and harmful desires
that plunge people into ruin and destruction. For the
love of money is a root of all kinds of evil, and in their
eagerness to be rich some have wandered away from
the faith and pierced themselves with many pains.

—I TIMOTHY 6:9–10

LET US PRAY

Our God, we bow before you and confess that we have, too often,
followed other gods, especially the god of money. Remind us, O
Lord, that the real problem is not money itself. Rather, it is the
love of money that can get us, and others, in real trouble. Forgive
us, Lord; help us be better stewards of the gifts you have given us.
And, thank you, God, for the gift of food. Help us find food for
those who have not. In Jesus' name. AMEN.

A Sincere Faith

I am reminded of your sincere faith, a faith that lived
first in your grandmother Lois and your mother
Eunice and now, I am sure, lives in you. For this
reason I remind you to rekindle the gift of God that is
within you through the laying on of my hands; for
God did not give us a spirit of cowardice, but rather a
spirit of power and of love and of self-discipline.

—2 TIMOTHY 1:5–7

LET US PRAY

God of all generations, we pause to give gratitude to you for all
those in the faith, who have passed that faith along to us. We
thank you for them, O lord, and we pray that we may be an
influence, for good, in the lives of those who come after us. In
Jesus' name. AMEN.

The Meaning of Faith

Now faith is the assurance of things hoped for, the
conviction of things not seen. Indeed, by faith our
ancestors received approval. By faith we understand
that the worlds were prepared by the word of God, so
that what is seen was made from things that are not
visible. —HEBREWS 11:1–3

LET US PRAY

Giver of every good and perfect gift, thank you for the gift of
faith. Faith for the living of our lives. Faith in people, faith in
promises made; faith that another day will come. But, most of all,
faith in you, O living and loving God. Thank you, God, for daily
nutrition. In Jesus' name. AMEN.

The Perfecter of Our Faith

Therefore, since we are surrounded by so great a cloud of witnesses, let us also lay aside every weight and the sin that clings so closely, and let us run with perseverance the race that is set before us, looking to Jesus the pioneer and perfecter of our faith, who for the sake of the joy that was set before him endured the cross, disregarding its shame, and has taken his seat at the right hand of the throne of God.

—HEBREWS 12:1–2

LET US PRAY

Mighty Forever God, we pause before you to give thanks for Jesus, the "pioneer and perfecter of our faith" who "endured the cross" for our sake that we might live as people of faith. Thanks be to you, Almighty God. In Jesus' name. AMEN.

Faith Without Works is Dead

What good is it, my brothers and sisters, if you say
you have faith but do not have works? Can faith save
you? If a brother or sister is naked and lacks daily
food, and one of you says to them, "Go in peace; keep
warm and eat your fill," and yet you do not supply
their bodily needs, what is the good of that? So faith
by itself, if it has no works, is dead. —JAMES 2:14–17

LET US PRAY

Proclaimer of justice, we confess that we have not always been
just in dealing with persons of poverty. It is so easy for us to think
that someone else will take care of them. Forgive us, O Lord, for
verbalizing our faith, but not always backing it up with action. O
God of holy love, may we practice a compassionate faith to those
in need. Thank you for the bread of life. In Jesus' name. AMEN.

SIX

God of Righteousness

Wisdom from Above

Who is wise and understanding among you? Show by
your good life that your works are done with
gentleness born of wisdom. But if you have bitter envy
and selfish ambition in your hearts, do not be boastful
and false to the truth. Such wisdom does not come
down from above, . . . But the wisdom from above is
first pure, then peaceable, gentle, willing to yield, full
of mercy and good fruits, without a trace of partiality
or hypocrisy. —JAMES 3:13–15, 17

LET US PRAY

O Fountain of wisdom, we pray that we may choose the right
kind of wisdom the "wisdom from above," as we deal with the
problems and decisions that come our way. Grant us, O Lord, the
wisdom to choose wisely. In Jesus' name. AMEN.

A Royal Priesthood

But you are a chosen race, a royal priesthood, a holy
nation, God's own people, in order that you may
proclaim the mighty acts of him who called you out of
darkness into his marvelous light.—I PETER 2:9

LET US PRAY

O High and Holy One, help us to understand what it means to be
a "chosen race, a royal priesthood, a holy nation." It does not mean
that we are better than anyone else. But it does mean that we are a
part of the church universal; and that we are now known as the
children of God. O Lord God, as children of the light, may we
proclaim your infinite love to all the world by words and deeds. In
Jesus' name. AMEN.

Speaking the Word of God

Above all, maintain constant love for one another, for
love covers a multitude of sins. Be hospitable to one
another without complaining. Like good stewards of the
manifold grace of God, serve one another with whatever
gift each of you has received. —I PETER 4:8–10

LET US PRAY

Source of health and strength, you have given us so many gifts,
gifts we can use as good stewards of all that has been given to us.
May we understand, O Lord, that the more we use our abilities
and skills to serve others, tells the world how much the love of
Christ is within us. Thank you, O gracious God, for this meal. In
Jesus' name. AMEN.

For Life and Godliness

[God's] divine power has given us everything needed for life and godliness, . . . For this very reason, you must make every effort to support your faith with goodness, and goodness with knowledge, and knowledge with self-control, and self-control with endurance, and endurance with godliness, and godliness with mutual affection, and mutual affection with love.

—2 Peter 1:3, 5–7

LET US PRAY

Thank you Lord, God, for these words from Second Peter: goodness . . . knowledge . . . self-control . . . endurance . . . godliness . . . mutual affection . . . love. We know what they mean, O Lord, so now we have no excuse for not putting them into action in our daily lives. And may your name be praised, Eternal Father-Mother-God. In Jesus' name. AMEN.

God is Love

Beloved, let us love one another, because love is from God; everyone who loves is born of God and knows God. Whoever does not love does not know God, for God is love. God's love was revealed among us in this way: God sent [Jesus] into the world so that we might live through him. In this is love, not that we loved God but that [God] loved us and sent [Jesus] to be the atoning sacrifice for our sins. Beloved, since God loved us so much, we also ought to love one another.

—1 JOHN 4:7–11

LET US PRAY

God of holy love, we come to you to confess that we have not always acted as if we loved you. We think of some of the things we have done, and ask for your forgiveness. Thank you, O God, for loving us before we loved you. And, thank you God for this meal before us. In Jesus' name. AMEN.

Because God First Loved Us

We love because [God] first loved us. Those who say,
"I love God,"' and hate their brothers or sisters, are
liars; for those who do not love a brother or sister
whom they have seen, cannot love God whom they
have not seen. The commandment we have from
[God] is this: those who love God must love their
brothers and sisters also. —1 JOHN 4:17, 19–21

LET US PRAY

Divine Creator, we come before you in humility and with a sense
of guilt, as we remember the times we have not loved those close
to us, or even those we call friends or associates. We have used
words that cut someone else sharply; and we have hurt others
through hateful action. O Lord, help us to do better than that
and to remember: "those who do not love a brother or sister
whom they have seen, cannot love God whom they have not
seen." In Jesus' name. AMEN.

What God Requires

With what shall I come before the Lord, and bow
myself before God on high? Shall I come before [God]
with burnt offerings, with calves a year old? . . . [God]
has told you, O mortal, what is good; and what does
the Lord require of you but to do justice, and to love
kindness, and to walk humbly with your God?

—MICAH 6:6, 8

LET US PRAY

Our gracious God, thank you for the prophet, Micah, who
chastised the people of Israel for their worship practices. He saw the
foolishness of bringing animals to be sacrificed on the altar; or even
worse, bringing children to "appease" you, O God, for the sins of
the people. Thank you, O Lord, for his telling the people what you
required: to treat everyone justly; to be kind to those you meet
along life's way; and to lead a humble life before God. AMEN.

Swords into Plowshares

[God] shall judge between the nations, and shall arbitrate for many peoples; they shall beat their swords into plowshares, and their spears into pruning hooks; nation shall not lift up sword against nation, neither shall they learn war any more. —ISAIAH 2:4

LET US PRAY

O God of peace, what great sorrow it must bring to you when you see nations at war with each other. And when you see so many of your people . . . men, women, and children . . . meet a terrible death. O Creator of all, our faith tells us that is not what you intended for your planet. May the nations come together, more and more, O Lord, that the prophet's vision may come true; and the nations shall not learn war anymore. And may all people have food adequate for their needs. In Jesus' name. AMEN.

The Glory of the Lord

A voice cries out: "In the wilderness prepare the way of the way of the Lord, make straight in the desert a highway for our God. Every valley shall be lifted up, and every mountain and hill be made low; the uneven ground shall become level, and the rough places a plain. Then the glory of the Lord shall be revealed, and all people shall see it together, for the mouth of the Lord has spoken." —ISAIAH 40:3–5

LET US PRAY

O God of Israel, how great was the expectation of those who waited to see the Lord. Through turmoil and suffering they looked for the day that you, Lord, would make all things right. Mountains, deserts, rough places would not keep you from appearing before them. And, then, your glory, O Lord, would be revealed to them. What a great day this would be! In your own way, O God, and in your own time, may it come. In Jesus' name. AMEN.

I Have Called You by Name

Do not fear, for I have redeemed you; I have called
you by name, you are mine. When you pass through
the waters, I will be with you; and through the rivers,
they shall not overwhelm you; when you walk through
fire you shall not be burned, and the flame shall not
consume you. For I am the Lord your God, the Holy
One of Israel, your Savior. —Isaiah 43:1–3

LET US PRAY

O God of knowledge, it is with complete trust that we know that
we are yours, that you know us by name . . . reminding us of
what Jesus said to his disciples long ago: "But even the hairs of
your head are all numbered. Fear not, therefore, you are of more
value than many sparrows" (Matthew 10:30–31). Through all the
tough times of our lives, help us to remember that you are the
Holy One, our Savior; and we are precious in your sight. Thank
you, God for the food that strengthens us. In Jesus' name. AMEN.

Seek the Lord

Seek the Lord while [the Lord] may be found, call upon [the Lord] while [the Lord] is near; let the wicked forsake their way, and the unrighteous their thoughts; let them return to the Lord, that [the Lord] may have mercy on them, and to our God, [who will] abundantly pardon. For my thoughts are not your thoughts, nor are your ways my ways, says the Lord. For as the heavens are higher than the earth, so are my ways higher than your ways and my thoughts than your thoughts. —ISAIAH 55:6–9

LET US PRAY

O God, at times we feel that you are far away from us, beyond the stars that are light years from us. Then it is that we know your ways or thoughts must be beyond all our imagining. On the other hand we feel you near to us when you invite us to seek you while you may be found. And it makes us feel that you care for us very much. Thanks be to you, O Lord! In Jesus' name. AMEN.

The Fast that I Choose

Is not this the fast that I choose: to loose the bonds of injustice, to undo the thongs of the yoke, to let the oppressed go free, and to break every yoke? Is it not to share your bread with the hungry, and bring the homeless poor into your house; when you see the naked, to cover them, and not to hide yourself from your own kin? . . . Then you shall call, and the Lord will answer; you shall cry for help, and [God] will say, Here I am. —ISAIAH 58:6–7, 9

LET US PRAY

O dear God, you make it very clear for us to understand just what real "fasting" is. It is not really about what you eat; or where you live. It is, rather, about helping people, whatever the need may be. O Lord, may we choose this "fast" we find in scripture. In Jesus' name. AMEN.

Loyalty and Faithfulness

Do not let loyalty and faithfulness forsake you; bind them around your neck, write them on the tablet of your heart. So you will find favor and good repute in the sight of God and of people. Trust in the Lord with all your heart, and do not rely on your own insight. In all your ways acknowledge [the Lord], and [the Lord] will make straight your paths. —PROVERBS 3:3–6

LET US PRAY

Dear God, how wonderful it is when there are persons we can depend upon as we go through life. Persons who are loyal and faithful in their relationships with other persons; and who have that same kind of relationship with you, Eternal God. Help us to "trust in you, O Lord, with all our heart." Thank you for the cuisine before us. In Jesus' name. AMEN.

The True Wealth

Happy are those who find wisdom, and those who get understanding, for her income is better than silver, and her revenue better than gold. She is more precious than jewels, and nothing you desire can compare with her. Long life is in her right hand; in her left hand are riches and honor. Her ways are ways of pleasantness, and all her paths are peace. —PROVERBS 3:13–17

LET US PRAY

Dear God, help us to understand that wisdom is far greater than any material possession. When we seek the ways of wisdom wonderful things can happen; and we are not at the mercy of others who would lead us elsewhere. Or are we at the mercy of pursuits that bring only devastation, tragedy, and no life at all. Enable us, O God, to choose wisdom as we make our decisions day by day. In Jesus' name. AMEN.

Speaking the Truth

Whoever speaks the truth gives honest evidence, but a false witness speaks deceitfully. Rash words are like sword thrusts, but the tongue of the wise brings healing. Truthful lips endure forever, but a lying tongue lasts only a moment. Deceit is in the mind of those who plan evil, but those who counsel peace have joy. —PROVERBS 12:17–20

LET US PRAY

God of truth, help us to think about what "lying lips" can do. They can get us into trouble; they can make us feel uneasy; they can hurt others; and they can get us into a habit of telling untruths, so we do not even think twice about it. Help us turn things around, and give us the courage to speak with "truthful lips." Thank you, Lord, for the food that nurtures us. In Jesus' name. AMEN.

A Gentle Tongue

A soft answer turns away wrath, but a harsh word stirs up anger. The tongue of the wise dispenses knowledge, but the mouths of fools pour out folly. The eyes of the Lord are in every place, keeping watch on the evil and the good. A gentle tongue is a tree of life, but perverseness in it breaks the spirit. —Proverbs 15:1–4

LET US PRAY

Dear God, we thank you for the ability to communicate with others, whether near or far, whether standing next to us, or halfway around the world. It is a gift that we should treasure. It is the gift of vocal chords, and an opening we call a "mouth." O God of compassion, love, and peace help us to think before we speak; to use our words in a way that will aid others, and make them feel good when they hear them. Our Lord, may a "gentle tongue" be our goal forever. In Jesus' name. Amen.

Love and Vegetables

Better is a little with the fear of the Lord than great treasure and trouble with it. Better is a dinner of vegetables where love is than a fatted ox and hatred with it. —PROVERBS 15:16–17

LET US PRAY

O God of hope and joy, it is not your will that those whom you have created should spend their lives in pain, in darkness, and in gloom. Some think, wrongly, that is the way you want it. O Radiant God, may our hearts and minds be tuned to the light of your Presence, that we may live in joy, in love, in peace. "Better is a dinner of vegetables where love is than a fatted ox and hatred with it." May love and joy live forever! In Jesus' name. AMEN.

The True Security

My child, do not let these escape from your sight:
keep sound wisdom and prudence, and they will be
life for your soul and adornment for your neck. Then
you will walk on your way securely and your foot will
not stumble. . . . for the Lord will be your confidence
and will keep your foot from being caught.

—PROVERBS 3:21–23, 26

LET US PRAY

Eternal God, you share your knowledge with us so that we may
make our way through this life, and have a strong sense of your
Presence, a strong sense of security. The scripture advises us that
we "keep sound wisdom and prudence." Thank you, O Lord, for
the gifts of each of these: wisdom, the ability to make judgments
based on sound knowledge, experience and understanding;
prudence, the ability to be cautious or discreet in conduct. Then,
we "will walk on our way securely." In Jesus' name. AMEN.

SEVEN

God of All Seasons

He Will Be Called Son of God

The angel said to her, "Do not be afraid, Mary, for you have found favor with God. And now, you will conceive in your womb and bear a son, and you will name him Jesus. . . . Mary said to the angel, "How can this be, since I am a virgin?" The angel said to her, "The Holy Spirit will come upon you, and the power of the Most High will overshadow you; therefore the child to be born will be holy; he will be called Son of God." —LUKE 1:30–31, 34–35

LET US PRAY

O gracious God, we come once again to celebrate the birth of Jesus. A holy child born in a cave. Not born to royalty, but to poor people. Thank you, Lord, for the baby, your Son, who grew up to be our Savior. O holy night, O night divine! In Jesus' name. AMEN.

Good News of Great Joy

Then an angel of the Lord stood before them, and the glory of the Lord shone around them, and they were terrified. But the angel said to them, "Do not be afraid; for see—I am bringing you good news of great joy for all the people: to you is born this day in the city of David a Savior, who is the Christ, the Lord. This will be a sign for you: you will find a child wrapped in bands of cloth and lying in a manger.

—LUKE 2:9–12

LET US PRAY

Mother-Father of our Lord Jesus Christ, we read this account of Jesus' birth, an account that has continued for centuries. And, yet, the great joy, the wonder of it all never ceases. O God, may the good news reach to every home and to every part of the globe, and may we never forget what "came upon the midnight clear." In Jesus' name. AMEN.

Hosanna in the Highest Heaven!

Then they brought the colt to Jesus and threw their cloaks on it; and he sat on it. Many people spread their cloaks on the road, and others spread leafy branches that they had cut in the fields. Then those who went ahead and those who followed were shouting, "Hosanna! Blessed is the one who comes in the name of the Lord! Blessed is the coming kingdom of our ancestor David! Hosanna in the highest heaven!" —MARK 11:7–10

LET US PRAY

Divine Creator, with the people who spread their cloaks before Jesus, we too lift our voices and shout out our Hosannas. Why not? The one who came riding on the lowly donkey was the one who was a great teacher; a divine healer; a friend of the poor, the outcasts, children; and our Redeemer. "Hosanna in the highest heaven!" AMEN.

The Crucifixion of Jesus

It was nine o'clock in the morning when they crucified
him. The inscription of the charge against him read,
"The King of the Jews." And with him they crucified
two bandits, one on his right and one on his left.
Those who passed by derided him, shaking their heads
and saying, "Aha! You who would destroy the temple
and build it in three days, save yourself, and come
down from the cross!" In the same way the chief
priests, along with the scribes, were also mocking him
among themselves and saying, "He saved others; he
cannot save himself. Let the Messiah, the King of
Israel, come down from the cross now, so that we may
see and believe." —Mark 15:25–32

LET US PRAY

God of sorrow, hear us as we bring our confession of sin before
you. Jesus died for us; for all who open their hearts and minds to
him. Forgive us, O God, for taking Jesus' sacrifice so lightly. Help
us realize what he endured, so that we might be reconciled to
you, O living God. In Jesus' name. Amen.

The Resurrection of Jesus

After the sabbath, as the first day of the week was
dawning, Mary Magdalene and the other Mary went
to see the tomb. And suddenly there was a great
earthquake; for an angel of the Lord, descending from
heaven, came and rolled back the stone and sat on it.
His appearance was like lightning, and his clothing
white as snow. For fear of him the guards shook and
became like dead men. But the angel said to the
women, "Do not be afraid; I know that you are
looking for Jesus who was crucified. He is not here;
for he has been raised, as he said. Come, see the place
where he lay. Then go quickly and tell his disciples,
'He has been raised from the dead.'"

—MATTHEW 28:1–7

LET US PRAY

Redeeming God, we lift joyful hearts to you because Christ is
risen. Even as our souls were in spiritual agony as we faced the
crucifixion of our Lord, so, now, our hearts are filled with joy as
we celebrate, with millions of persons, his resurrection. And, we
remember those glorious words of Paul: "But thanks be to God
who gives us the victory through our Lord Jesus Christ"
(Romans 15:57). In Jesus' name. AMEN.

Peace be with You

Jesus came and stood among them and said, "Peace be with you." After he said this, he showed them his hands and his side. Then the disciples rejoiced when they saw the Lord. Jesus said to them again, "Peace be with you. As [God] has sent me, so I send you." When he had said this, he breathed on them and said to them, "Receive the Holy Spirit. If you forgive the sins of any, they are forgiven them; if you retain the sins of any, they are retained." —JOHN 20:19–23

LET US PRAY

God of wonders, how filled with joy the disciples must have been when Jesus came into their upper room, and showed himself to them. In one moment deep sadness was turned into absolute elation. They thought he was gone from them forever. Now, he was with them, and their world was right. And to add ecstasy to joy, O God, Jesus breathed on them your Holy Spirit; and they were now ambassadors, witnessing a new faith to the world. O Lord, make us ambassadors too. In Jesus' name. AMEN.

Memorial Day

When your children ask in time to come, "What do
these stones mean to you?" then you shall tell them
that the waters of the Jordan were cut off in front of
the ark of the covenant of the Lord. When it crossed
over the Jordan, the waters of the Jordan were cut off.
So these stones shall be to the Israelites a memorial
forever.—JOSHUA 4:6B–7

LET US PRAY

O God, we come before you in these moments to remember
those who have gone before us, whom we loved so much, and
whose departure from our midst still gives us a deep sorrow. And
yet there is more than the sorrow, because we know that they are
in your hands, O God, and are recipients of your eternal love.
We also pause to remember those who have given the last full
measure of devotion on behalf of country, of freedom. May our
gratitude, O God, never end. Each time we look, with love, upon
a cross; upon a star of David; upon whatever our "stones," that
will be to us "a memorial forever." In Jesus' name. AMEN.

The Great Commission

And Jesus came and said to them [the disciples], "All authority in heaven and on earth has been given to me. Go therefore and make disciples of all nations, baptizing them in the name of the [Parent] and of the Son and of the Holy Spirit, and teaching them to obey everything that I have commanded you. And, remember, I am with you always, to the end of the age."—MATTHEW 28:18–20

LET US PRAY

O ever loving God, open our minds and our hearts to the words of The Great Commission. Help us to understand that disciples are persons who want to share the good news of Jesus Christ with others. And we can do that because the risen Christ is with us always, to guide and to empower. All glory and dominion, wisdom and power be yours, O God, forever more. In Jesus' name. AMEN.